A Graceless & Flourishing Heart

A Poetry Collection

LAUREN EVE

Dedicated to...

B

For every slow burn moment
& every mile travelled
you changed everything x

———

Contents

———

Graceless

When some people
prepare for battle
they sharpen their knives
organise their armoury
but I choose words
ready for your shrapnel
every confidence
reconfigured for pain
but I will rise above
because without you
I became stronger
realised I was worthy
of more than being your
emotional punch bag
instead I'm ready
for all conflictions
I am my own
emotional heroine.

———

First loves
are broken bouquets
handled so daintily
held aloft to
simply be admired
until the blooms
wilt out of water
no longer idealised
only good for
the captured moment
of fleeting florescence.

———

If good is evil
and love is hate
am I in your
heart always?

Cute but never fierce
radiant and broken down
sweet not overtly strong
say you're innocent
they'll say you're wrong
fly high yet tethered
smile in public
he won't ask twice
cry alone
under dim bedroom lights
It girl for a day
you're nothing new.

———

Don't stand in the shade
that they create
don't listen to the lies
they tend and cultivate
leave that damaged earth
to those who made it dark and drained

Do blossom and grow
from roots of your own
do bend in the gentle breeze
your beauty fully revealed
allow and embrace that chance
of what can and what will
a precious moment to
know your value
and breathe new life
into seeing you're perfectly you.

———

We the broken hearted
sew the two halves
glue the shards
collect the fragments
gather the dust
   we rebuild
   we restart
   we revive ourselves
      we're stronger than you'll ever know.

Berate me
breathe into me
leave me
love me
easy on me
everything within me.

———

I'm the type of girl
whose head
is buried in a book
or lost in the clouds
but I never let myself
get lost completely
because pages can
be ripped and torn
and storm clouds
threaten from above
it's better to know
dreams are just as
beautifully fragile
as paper and air.

———

They never tell you
being in love
can be a lonely affair.

Graceless regrets die on my lips
days ever absent of your touch
forgotten secrets that we shared
endless hours before the dawn
so blinded by your charms
your words lose their power
as the ink dried on paper
when the sunlight breaks through
your laughter forever altered
now becomes a mournful sound
You're someone else's love.

———

Displaced by my identity
distrusting of my feelings
destroyed by my past
detached from the truth
so I act grateful for you.

Her voice cracks as
she puts her deep secrets
her painful truths
out into the world
to be judged and discussed
heckled by strangers
but loved by some...
forever and always
so painfully human.

———

Plan A
didn't work out
'the first is the strongest'
people say
but I learnt more
I made my way beyond
to the next
and found what I wanted
never knew I needed
no plan just a step
towards B...

———

I am that girl
who conceals
parts of herself
hidden in amongst
those you never forget
I'm just a girl
whose not used
to being missed.

I could say
we had fun
and end it there
I could leave
and remember you
with an honest smile
but I want
to revisit your kiss
constantly
I already need
the sound of your laugh
endlessly
as
you changed me
irrevocably.

———

Life is for living
so just reach out...
it all sounds so simple
but in reality
my heart drags down my sleeve
its broken edges scratching
at frayed skin
until the pain is soothed
by a few simple words
a beautiful smile
the tender promise of hope
you ease my burdens
and bind my wounds
reaching out for you
as natural as breathing
and if I don't overthink
life becomes more than living.

———

Inadequacy
was never the feeling
of being alone
when I was with you.

She switched
drinks to tequila
in March
quoting drunken dreams
but he aimed
to keep it casual
She changed
from Vans to Docs
in May
playing groupie
but then her band
got too good a deal
She swore off
all technology
in September
taking up meditation
but their phone
revealed extensive lies
She laughs off
how she absorbs
month after month
something from another
pushing aside
what makes her
incredible
everyday of the year.

———

My chest hollowed out
a grand oak with no sun
swamped by the dreaded dark
I have no place to fall
only to wither where I stand.

———

They can call me reckless
or sweetly naive for
still running to you when
we may not be forever
and you might say goodbye
it's pointless to pretend
to think things through
when I'll choose this
and your kiss every time.

———

Regretful

I wrote something today
a thought I may read years from now
and I know it won't burn
and tear me apart
like it does right now
and I know it won't fill my throat
with sheer effort not to cry
and it won't feel like my heart
is strained against the vice around it

and in years to come
what you did to me
will be a distant memory
a long lost story
a cautionary tale of trust
as I write this today I know
that you could never be forgotten
that your words cannot be contained
by the pages of my journal

they spilled out onto my skin
your actions forever marking
the porcelain you used to graze
you chipped away at all the good
so I wrote this aware of all the lies you told
aware that it meant nothing
and all I can do is try to carry on
and one day it might hurt less to breathe
like it does right now.

———

I broke all of my traditions for you
every superstition seemed worth the risk
because you broke the mould of
everything I expected love to be.

If it were all so easy
my heart wouldn't burn
from trying to carry on
loving you
losing you
forgetting you
and when all that's left is ashes
saying 'no' to you
next time you decide
to pick me up
where you left me ablaze.

———

My fingerprints trailed across the pictures that dyed her skin
dark swirls of grey and charcoal lines which reconstructed memories
of places and people along her way
would I one day leave a permanent touch upon her body?
one exposed soul?
an open book if you read the language in which she lives
her experiences of love and pain
indelible in ink
a body awash with years of longing
carvings of adventure into her flesh
for a body so adept to permanence
she is fleeting to me
a blink in time and she is gone...
for a moment
until her form appears to me once more...
a figure made more of canvas than skin.

———

I can't do that
I can't do anything
I can't stop anything
I won't stop anything
You won't stop anything.

Turns out
my bad habit
is saying 'don't worry'
cause I do for you
is uttering 'it's fine'
when it hurts me
is reassuring 'it's okay'
although it's far from
it turns out
my bad habit is you.

———

If I had known
our end at
the beginning
would I have
walked away
ran until the
breath left my body?
would I have been
honest with myself
acknowledging
all the tiny pieces
of me that would
be taken
never to be returned?
parts of me wish
I'd have turned those pages
back to front
but to start at the end
would have meant
no beginning
for who I became
in spite of loving you.

———

Your two sides
drew me in
but now I'm
on the inside
I don't know
if this or that
is the real you
and well my
heart sinks
when you flirt
with her
and my mind flips
trying to unravel
where I should stand
as you revolve
between your
dual selves.

————

Outed
ousted
alone
afraid
every
emotion
  I...
have no words
only scars.

Memories are malleable
depending on the day
you can be
everything I ever wanted
but walked away from
or you are
everything I hated about
being kept secret.

———

Lauren Eve

I might lose you tomorrow
but I'll love you forever today.

I gave you it all
every breath
every piece of skin
every dignity
I ever earnt
being the good girl
doing the right thing
but your look
your touch
ebbed away
at my sanity
my safe little world
was yours to destroy
to pick apart
with fingernails indenting
my porcelain shell
red streaks marking
what was yours
but I took me back
every breath
every piece of skin
every dignity
I ever regained for myself.

———

Her words
touch you
like no hand has
she makes you feel
like it's all true
and tangible
something real
a fiction to grasp.

Inexplicable worry
unexpected anxiety
implausible thoughts
but unbelievable serenity
all because of you.

———

Life was simple
myself not a priority
but an existence
then you made me smile...

Hips pressed against hips
hands holding your neck
your kiss is my new addiction
with every taste and pull closer
I know I'm getting in too deep
rationality ebbing with every fix.

———

Hopeful

Dancing in your kitchen
standing on your toes
drinking wine by the fire
dropping glasses to the ground
kissing you as I fall asleep
holding me slightly too tight
imperfectly wonderful
perfectly us.

———

The way you look at me
is like I have never been seen before
a girl in the background
reimagined as more than just a woman
you mean more to me
that my quiet heart could ever beat for.

Gold and purple beads scattered
on the sidewalk of New Orleans
abandoned cocktail glasses
left in that hipster bar in Zurich
a forgotten paperback half
in the sands of Como's beach
remnants of us remain
everywhere but here.

———

I just wanted
to put love
out in the world
but I knew it
would never be returned.

When the rain pours
and a chill settles
in the late summer air
leaves fall like petals
wrapped in your arms
safety replaces every care.

———

Entwining your fingers in mine
leading towards the inevitable
after late night conversations
pictures with motives unfiltered
inhibitions draped like fabric
dropped away with intention.

———

'I care'
two simple words
an utterance to
stun you
stop you
where you stand
given out to the world
with true conviction
you hoped
but never believed
she would declare it
to you
and your fractured soul.

———

I have so many secrets
that cower underneath my tears
a multitude of worries
boundless trappings of fear
I tell my truths to the wind
placing all that remains
in your open hands
expecting you to disappear
yet you stay and ask to understand.

She infuses
depths and meaning
into simple words
guided feelings
your soul altered
it rises to the surface
with space to flourish
your purpose amended
finally awash with the
emotions you mislaid.

———

Kiss me on the pavement
lace hands on the sidewalk
hold me close in the autumn
into your world I'll fall.

Protect your heart
shield your soul
hide your light
make them comfortable
push your truth down
but what if you
let your heart soar
allowed your soul to sing
shone your light in full spectrum
refractions of glorious colour?
in vibrant shades of hope
saturated hues of love
exposed to acceptance
your truth set free to feel
the iridescent swell of Pride.

———

Aching to believe in you
in something far greater
than the smile you curate
gripping tight to a hidden truth.

Wait for
that person
who you can't wait
to message
'good morning'
but never utter
'good night'.

———

Another envelope
no ink upon paper
but still the letters
stay bold with promise
stark with desire
frequented by
...
that says you
wait for me
as much as
I long for you.

———

For those days
when her voice
is all you need.

It's not about that kiss
it's not about their touch
it's about finding that
somebody who helps
you become happier
within yourself
it's about letting someone
build you up to a level
of contentment
because to them
you are more than enough
it's about being with
that one who will always
add more to your heart
than they will ever take
for me that's what
love is about.

———

You can fix
anything
with your two hands
piece all things
back together again
just like you
fixed me
when I believed
I was beyond repair.

———

Soft skin
lost in sheets
finding you
in the dark
forever
the place
I want to be.

Meeting you was always
going to be bittersweet
an emotional pivot
attempting to keep momentum
without moving too fast
away from expectations
towards the evolution
of our ambivalent meeting.

———

When you know Home has been altered
from the place you thought you belonged.

If you want this
fight for me
I don't want you
running in the rain
I don't need you
holding up the boombox
I don't have to see you
dance to a brass band
I just want you to care
enough to hold my hand
and ask me to stay.

———

She swept
a wayward curl
behind my ear
    before
her fingertips
gently traced
my exposed neck
    before
she replaced
every single thought
in my tired mind
    before
    I fell.

——

Flourishing

Your delicate protection
forever arching over
those who will
always have pieces
of your heart
their voices scattered
amongst the willows
but shared memories
never to be parted
a once tough exterior
etched away to a
stunning beauty inside.

———

I sleep easier
knowing that
I have someone
more beautiful
than any dream.

You're good with the slow burn
but my heart beats differently
my mind blazes with possibilities
I restrain my choice of words
to avoid igniting us
before we even have time to begin.

A world lockdown
led me to you
in a universe
that was frozen
you melted
my barricades
and unlocked
emotions that
travelled further
than I ever
dreamed I could.

———

If you can tell
I'm upset from a text
then you have me read
if you ask me 'what's wrong?'
then you have my mind
if you ask to call
then you have my heart.

Life might just be
a series of moments
of joy and pain
made up of people
who enter your world
with the potential
of permanence
or of minimal touch

but you make every
moment something
I want to grasp
and hold to my chest
to blink and frame
every conversation
to save every song
knotting each lyric to us

to attempt to contain
every shared experience
in the thumbed pages
of my well travelled journal
your name repeated in ink
more familiar than my own
you've made every moment
a chance to truly live.

———

I want pancakes
on sunday morning
I never want us
to finish an entire film
I want to make us
chicory spiked coffees
I never want to wake
next to anyone but you.

———

The soft cotton
of your shirt
upon my skin
plaid on pale
feels like home.

Midnight
and beyond
light all gone
your fingertips
burn my skin
I crave it all
scorch the sheets
ashen my body
blazing together
you ignite my soul.

———

The way you reach for my hand out in the street
the way you kiss me when we reach a stoplight
the way you smile when we're making coffee
the way you tell me 'we'll figure it out'
the way you let me into your world
lets me know everything unsaid.

———

The flowers you bought me
were so vibrant
so bold at telling everyone
who glanced over
that you were waiting
for someone worthy
of a delicate sacrifice
that those softening buds
were to be gifted
to someone you cannot
stop thinking about
that those stems should
be passed from your hand
to signify that friendship
is less than what we are
but announced love
might not be too much
one day long
after those petals
have fallen and
our new season has begun.

———

An ocean
is not so far
to travel
when your touch
feels so much
like home.

I travel light these days
choosing to donate
pass along things
that don't mean
quite so much anymore
they don't give me
comfort or peace
in a place that
doesn't feel quite
so much like home
I prefer the lightness
the relief of a little
less to carry on
I don't mind living
out of a suitcase
because you gave me
a few items in a drawer
a shelf that could be
all mine
I don't care how
long the trip takes
how quickly I must
run for a connection
in another new place
because I'm almost there
I travel light these days
my heart the lightest of all.

———

In the morning light
I lie in your arms
you grace my cheek
with a gentle kiss
as our bodies fit
so effortlessly
together under
your crumpled sheets.

————

Slow me down
keep me safe
correct my assumptions
hold me close
I believe you
would never
could never
want to hurt me.

I keep putting me in your future
and not letting us grow into our own
the partnership we can become
I don't want to waste a moment
by looking out towards
a potential horizon
a dream I'll still hold
but tucked in my pocket
instead of stitched
upon my sleeve.

———

People say it was romantic
our story of the whirlwind
the first meeting in Europe
travelling through
beautiful landscapes
laughing over
incredible food
stolen kisses in
crowds of strangers
but all I could take in
was every breathtaking
reality of finally
breathing the same air.

———

You took me out of myself
I am out of the shadows
and finally in the sunlight
but I stand on my own
proud and blossoming
evermore.

I wear a golden heart
that cracked today
without warning
an embellishment
wrapped around
my smallest finger
I hope it is
not an omen
just a minor shift
in something fragile
a warning to fortify
for things to come.

———

Love is when
the everyday feels like everything.

Lauren Eve

I sense happiness today
in cold blasts of air
on my winter kissed skin
in fresh perfume scents
of springtime blooms
in sun dappled mornings
too hot and too early to wake
in the crinkle of fall leaves
that blanket the ground
give me any season for
I can flourish and thrive in all.

———

She makes my heart full
my days longer
the nights endless
I could waste an eternity
just loving her.

———

Acknowledgements

For everyone in the book community who gave me a place to grow, I
can never fully say how grateful I am.
For all the incredible and talented women I now consider my friends,
I have learnt so many invaluable lessons.
For my friends and family who never gave up on me.
And thank you times a million for anyone who reads this collection
and can relate to the joy and pain we go through everyday.

Love is never easy but learning to love yourself, even a little, is the
most graceless and most beautiful of things.

Thank you all again, Lauren Eve.

———

About The Author

Lauren Eve became a poet by accident through late night posts and is currently writing her debut novel. She is an avid reader and reviewer of all genres, but has a soft spot of Sapphic romances and YA thrillers. Lauren studied English Literature at University but often still writes on scraps of paper and phone memos. When her world isn't focused on books she can be found crafting or living out of a suitcase.

Instagram @laureneve_books

———

Printed in Great Britain
by Amazon

17083842R00056